THE TRUTH ABOUT
BUTTERFLIES

Maxwell Eaton III

ROARING BROOK PRESS

NEW YORK

Copyright © 2020 by Maxwell Eaton III
Published by Roaring Brook Press
Roaring Brook Press is a division of Holtzbrinck
Publishing Holdings Limited Partnership
120 Broadway, New York, NY 10271
The art for this book was created using pen and ink with digital coloring.
mackids.com

Library of Congress Control Number: 2019948798
ISBN: 978-1-250-23253-3

Our books may be purchased in bulk for promotional, educational, or business use. Please
contact your local bookseller or the Macmillan Corporate and Premium Sales Department at
(800) 221-7945 ext. 5442 or by email at MacmillanSpecialMarkets@macmillan.com.

First edition, 2020
Book design by Jennifer Browne

Printed in China by Shaoguan Fortune Creative Industries Co. Ltd.,
Shaoguan, Guangdong Province

1 3 5 7 9 10 8 6 4 2

These are butterflies.
Butterflies are a type of colorful flying insect.

There are more than 18,000 butterfly species. They live all over the world and come in countless shapes, sizes, and colors.

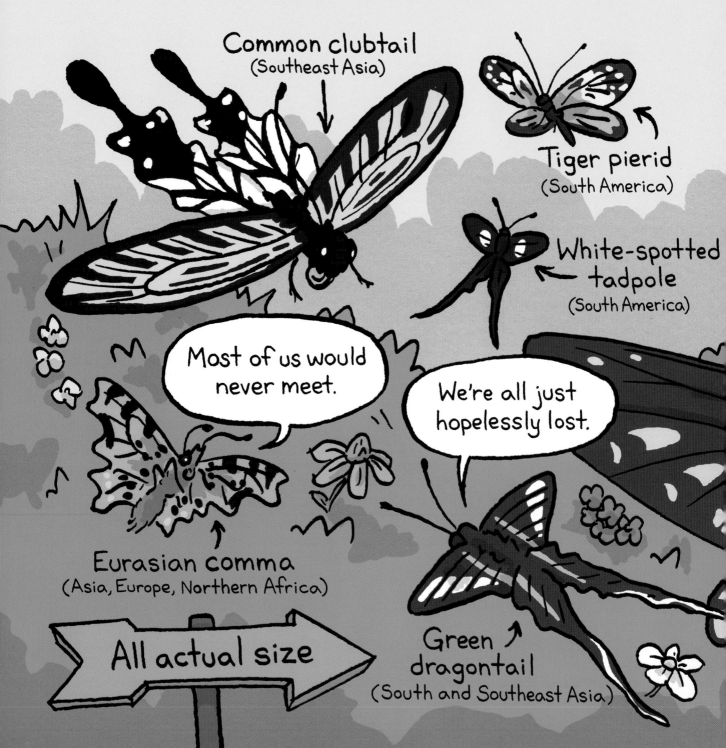

Butterflies are known for their incredible wings. Along with flying and finding mates, each species uses its wings to avoid being eaten by larger predators like birds, snakes, frogs, toads, and lizards.

Speaking of look-alikes, butterflies are closely related to moths, but there are some common differences.

THE WINGS OF BOTH BUTTERFLIES AND MOTHS ARE COVERED WITH MILLIONS OF TINY SCALES. THERE MAY BE AS MANY AS 125,000 SCALES IN THE SQUARE BELOW.

Dull colors

Dull? I'm the life of the party!

"Feathered" antennae

Robust body

Poplar hawkmoth (Europe and Asia)

Active at night

Rests with wings folded across back or out to sides

Moth

Most adult butterflies feed on nectar, a sugary liquid made by flowers. The butterfly uses its proboscis [pro-boss-is] like a straw to slurp it up.

Orange is my favorite flavor.

Proboscis

Coneflower

Tiger swallowtail

Oh, don't look so shocked.

SOME BUTTERFLIES SIP LIQUIDS FROM TREE WOUNDS, DECAYING FRUIT, ANIMAL FECES (POOP), OR ROTTING ANIMALS.

Hackberry

BUTTERFLIES ARE AGILE AND DELICATE BUT THEY DON'T START LIFE THAT WAY. THEY GO THROUGH A PROCESS CALLED METAMORPHOSIS WHERE THEIR BODIES TRANSFORM AS THEY GROW. FOR ALL BUTTERFLIES, IT HAPPENS IN FOUR STAGES. LET'S FOLLOW A MONARCH THROUGH THE STAGES!

The Egg (Ovum)

An adult female butterfly lays a fertilized egg on a plant that its young can eat. This Monarch chooses a milkweed plant.

A MONARCH FEMALE LAYS EACH EGG INDIVIDUALLY BUT WILL DO THIS HUNDREDS OF TIMES.

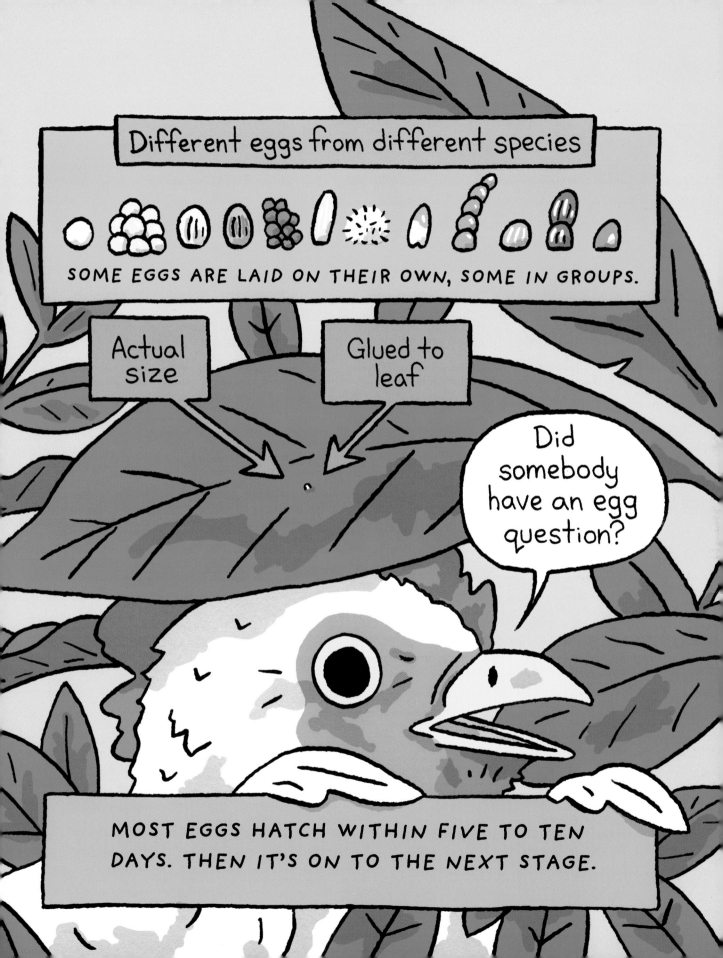

The egg hatches and out crawls a tiny caterpillar. This monarch caterpillar will spend the next two to three weeks eating milkweed leaves and growing.

Molting

A CATERPILLAR'S SKIN, CALLED THE CUTICLE, DOESN'T STRETCH. IN ORDER TO GROW, THE CATERPILLAR MAKES A NEW, LARGER SKIN UNDER ITS OLD ONE. THEN IT CRAWLS OUT OF THE OLD SKIN AND EATS IT! THIS IS CALLED MOLTING AND HAPPENS UP TO FIVE TIMES DURING THE LARVA STAGE.

Old skin

* Never disturb a molting caterpillar.

Caterpillars are soft and slow, so, like adult butterflies, they have a few tricks to avoid being eaten.

Who'd want to eat me?

I'm poisonous.

Monarch

I have weird, smelly, red glands.

Giant swallowtail

I'm difficult to swallow.

Zebra longwing

I look like a snake.

Spicebush swallowtail

I look like bird poop.

Viceroy

Mission accomplished. I'm sick.

AFTER TWO TO FOUR WEEKS OF NONSTOP EATING, IT'S TIME FOR THE CATERPILLAR TO MOLT ONE LAST TIME.

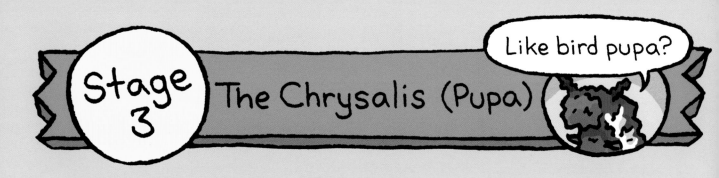

Like bird pupa?

The caterpillar will shed its skin once more, but this time under the cuticle is a hard case called the chrysalis. Here's how the monarch does it:

I weave some silk to hang from while the chrysalis forms under my skin.

Fourteen hours later the chrysalis is ready and my skin splits open.

Silk

When I shed, the couch gets covered with fur.

Stage 4 — The Adult Butterfly

Oooh, the suspense!

The final transformation! After ten to fifteen days inside the chrysalis, the newly formed adult butterfly is ready to emerge. This can take a few hours.

Monarch chrysalis becomes clear the day before emerging.

Chrysalis cracks open and butterfly crawls out.

Hi.

Hangs upside-down and pumps blood into crumpled wings.

But before she can lay eggs, our butterfly will need to find a mate. Luckily, male butterflies are on the lookout, as well. They have two strategies for searching.

A few hours after finding each other, the female flies off to lay eggs.

In many places, cold winters can interrupt this cycle. Some butterflies simply die with the freezing weather. Others survive the winter by hibernating like bears.

BUTTERFLIES MAY SPEND THE WINTER AS ADULTS OR CATERPILLARS OR IN CHRYSALIS FORM DEPENDING ON THE SPECIES.

Monarchs avoid the cold altogether. Like many birds, they migrate and make long journeys south. Monarchs in the northeast of North America fly as far as 2,500 miles to a small area in the mountains of central Mexico.

Did anyone save me a spot?

THEY GROUP TOGETHER OR ROOST ON OYAMEL FIR TREES WHERE THEY DO LITTLE BUT REST UNTIL SPRING WHEN THEY JOURNEY BACK NORTH TO MATE AND LAY EGGS.

Of course, there is one threat that butterflies can't escape no matter how far they fly. Humans are causing a decline in many species and causing others to go extinct.

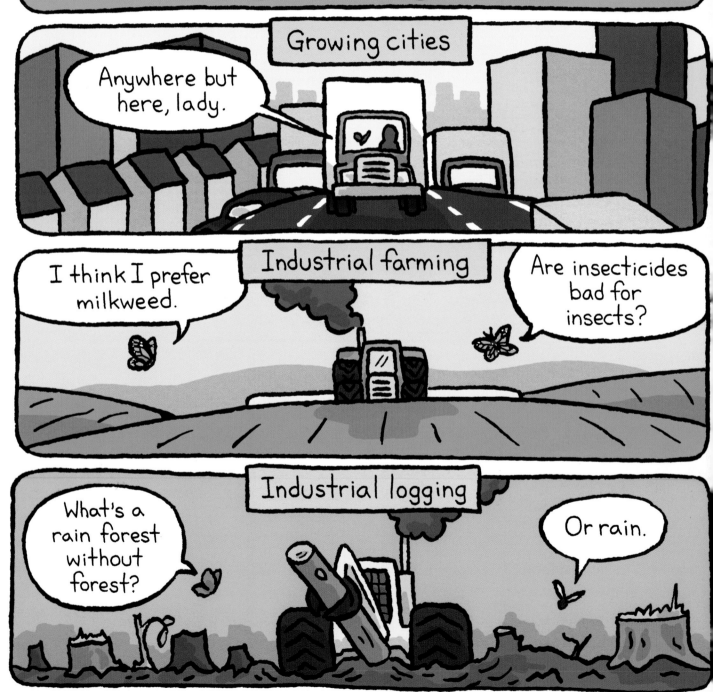

The good news is you can begin to help by learning more about butterflies, teaching others, and even giving butterflies a place to live.

CREATING A BUTTERFLY GARDEN CAN BE AS SIMPLE AS LETTING A PIECE OF LAWN GROW WILD WITH "WEEDS."

ANOTHER WAY TO LEARN MORE AND HELP IS TO RAISE WILD BUTTERFLIES FROM EGGS OR CATERPILLARS. HERE ARE THE BASICS OF RAISING MONARCHS FROM CATERPILLARS.

Start looking in a milkweed patch a week after seeing the first monarch of spring.

There we go.

Chewed leaves

Frass (caterpillar poop)

The caterpillar is found. Cut the leaf it's on, and place it in a clean plastic container.

I was in the middle of something.

Cut a bunch of leaves to feed the caterpillar later.

Wrap in damp paper towel.

Put in plastic bag in fridge.*

*Will keep for a few days

Caution! Wash hands after handling. Leaf sap irritates skin.

Place the container in a bright place but away from direct sunlight (and cats).

I dare you.

Once a day, remove the leaf with the caterpillar on it. Dump frass and old leaves. Add fresh leaves. Put the caterpillar back and snap on the lid.

I love a clean home.

But remember, never disturb a molting caterpillar!

Collect fresh milkweed leaves as needed.

Snip Snip

The caterpillar will form a chrysalis on the lid within two weeks.

Patience, please.

In a week or two the adult butterfly will emerge. Again, do not disturb.

Where's that cat?

Once the butterfly starts to flutter its wings (a few hours after emerging) it's ready to be released.

Safe travels!

I give up.

I knew there was more to life than Tupperware!

Ahem.

WELL DONE! EVERY BUTTERFLY COUNTS.

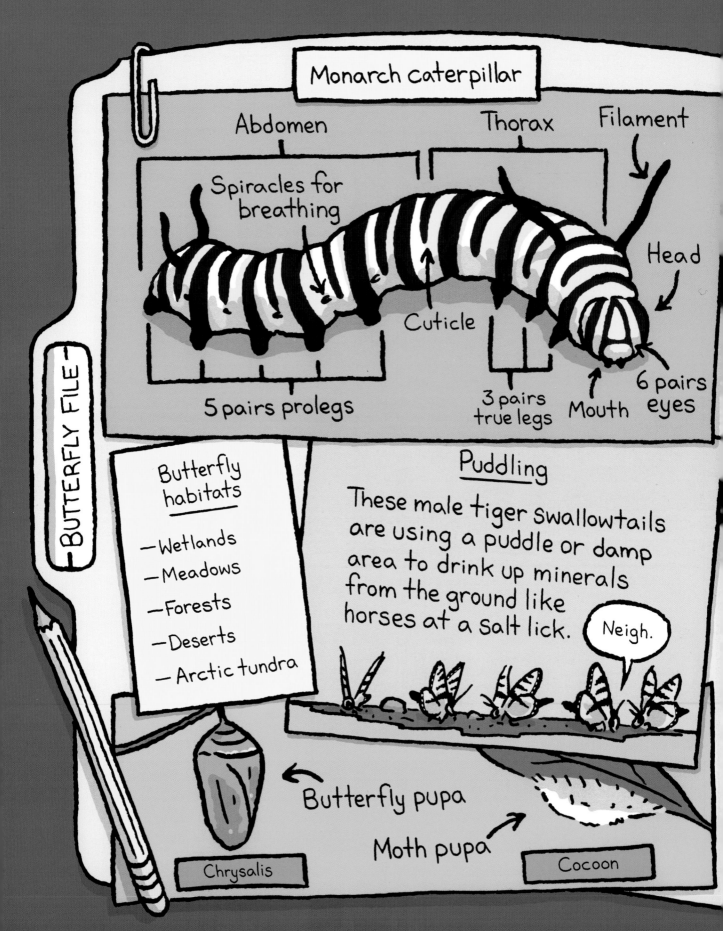

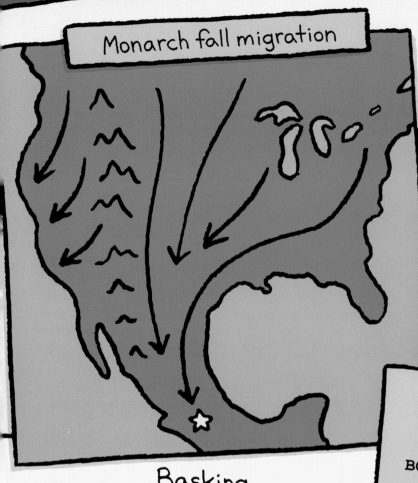

Monarch fall migration

A common caterpillar defense. Curl up and drop to ground.

Basking

— Can't move much below 50°F
— Need warmth to fly
— Will perch and use scales on wings to absorb heat from sun

Further Research

BOOKS FOR LARVA

How to Raise Monarch Butterflies, Carol Pasternak, Firefly Books, 2012.

The Life Cycles of Butterflies, Janet Schulman, Judy Burris, and Wayne Richards, Storey Publishing, 2006.

BOOKS FOR ADULTS

Monarchs and Milkweed: A Migrating Butterfly, a Poisonous Plant, and Their Remarkable Story of Coevolution, Anurag Agrawal, Princeton University Press, 2017.

National Audubon Society Field Guide to North American Butterflies, Robert Michael Pyle, Alfred A. Knopf, 1981.